The Epistle of Philippians
Mirror Bible by François du Toit

& The Law of Three
by Bob Mumford

LIFECHANGERS®

P.O. Box 3709 ❖ Cookeville, TN 38502
931.520.3730 ❖ lc@lifechangers.org

PLUMBLINE

Published by:

LIFECHANGERS ®
L I B R A R Y S E R I E S

P.O. Box 3709 | Cookeville, TN 38502
(800) 521-5676 | www.lifechangers.org

All Rights Reserved
ISBN 978-1-940054-18-6

© 2018 Lifechangers
All Rights Reserved
Printed in the United States of America

Introduction to Philippians & The Law of Three

By Bob Mumford

It is both a joy and a challenge to introduce you to an innovative and fresh translation of the New Testament. It is not bound by overt doctrinal and denominational presuppositions. This renewed translation has served to enlighten and encourage us in ways that seemed to make it compulsory for us to make it known to you. With careful consideration, we have chosen Paul's *Letter to the Philippians*. It may serve as one of the more Christ-centering of the prison Epistles. With great care and unusual boldness, this author, François du Toit who lives in South Africa, seeks to introduce us to the authentic Jesus Paul was seeking to make known to the Philippian believers.

There are two words that are biblically attached to the idea of Agape that help define what it means to follow Jesus. Those words are spontaneity and risk. The Lord takes risk, and as a direct result of the journey, we here at Lifechangers have been making needed adjustments. We have chosen to embrace that spiritual change is inexorable.

Judith and I have come to know Francois and his wife personally, understand their biblical presuppositions and have, with joy, engaged the Mirror Bible gaining personal insight and added understanding of the Kingdom. Francois implements both spontaneity and risk as he boldly translates the contours of this amazing letter of life and compassion.

This Plumbline promises to draw you out into a new and garden-fresh grasp of the biblical Greek and its intent to provide God the Father His Own inheritance. Sheer spontaneity in translation will take your breath away! It will, I promise you, also cause you be required to take the risk needed to begin to see and embrace the issues as they unfold. If some are too "demanding," put them in the pantry for further investigation!

Carefully evaluate the implications, and when you are persuaded, allow the Lord to "move the furniture in your basement". You will discover, with joy, that this response will become necessary as you are re-introduced to concepts that you thought you knew! It is risky. You will be glad that you had the courage to take the risk.

The Law of Three

All events in life, none accepted, are planned and executed on the principle of the "Law of Three". It actually goes like this:

1. I am going to wash the car: needed preparation and planning.
2. The car is now washed: the act/project has been completed.
3. Clean up the area to finish: put away tools, wrap up the details.

To my own personal and theological surprise, I am now discovering that this is the manner in which God as Creator and Father has prepared and executed His own agenda. The Greek word for Father's agenda or purpose is *boulema*. It signifies God's fixed and determined purpose. The original depth of this marvelous word can best be expressed as Father's affectionate desire and deliberate resolve to accomplish the "act or project" that He has planned from before the foundation of the world.

In God's Own "Law of Three," clear steps were taken in Eternity to prepare for and execute the redemptive act of Jesus Christ becoming incarnate and the completion of: "It is Finished." We are called to participate in the third stage: clean up the remaining details and make all the area complete and restored. This is the "Law of Three" in the larger redemptive act of God t bringing to completion all that He has promised: "In you, Abraham, all of the families of the earth shall be blessed" (Genesis 22:18). Abraham's promise has become a Person, the incarnate Person of our Lord Jesus Christ.

There is then, as a result of the Law of Three, a presentation of three actual births. How beautiful and delightful. Note carefully each of the three:

1. We were chosen and birthed in Christ, before the world was formed. The presuppositional emphasis seeks to restore this original birth as our true identity: God brought us forth in eternity!

Then He planned to do so in time.

2. We were brought into the world by the natural birth of our mother. There was no other route.
3. We are offered the third birth, which is the new birth Jesus spoke to Nicodemus in John 3. God, as Father, is seeking to bring His family home to Himself.

What this Plumbline seeks to clearly present is that the Eternal Seed from which we were birthed in eternity is incorruptible. The serious changes and promised disruptions of Scripture, some past, some present and pressured, some yet to be embraced, will require our strengthened sense of God having finished His act/project in time. We are placing our faith and confidence in more than "religious experience." We rest in an eternal plan that precedes the very cosmos in which we now live.

ASSESS THE FIRST LAW OF THREE

There are 10 clear biblical events (presented later) that tell us how diligent God the Father was in preparation for the final and efficient accomplishment of His act of radical forgiveness for the whole world. They happened in eternity before the world began. What is being imparted by such prescient insight and precaution is the fact that God does know what He is doing.

I am eager for us to see clearly that Father God provided the cure prior to ever allowing the disease. Listen carefully and begin to allow it to soak in: "The

Lamb slain from the foundation of the world…" (Revelation 13:8). This compels us to understand God, as a Father, really is in charge of this entire confusing and complex set of circumstances!

ASSESS THE SECOND LAW OF THREE

The Redemptive act was accomplished before it was required. All scripture anticipated Christ's Blood being shed. All Old Testament sacrifice was based on the reality of that which was to happen in time: we are about to wash the car: the project for which we have prepared is now about to happen.

Time enables us to perceive the actual incarnation of the Son of God. All of the gospels tell us, in detail, the events of the redemptive act. His life, ministry, and living sacrifice all lead up to the redemptive act in time having been accomplished. His birth, death, resurrection, and ascension are understood as eternity being walked out in time. "It is finished" (John 19:30). The "act" has now been completed—nothing to be added and nothing has been omitted. All that was fully complete in eternity has now been made fully complete in time.

ASSESS THE THIRD LAW OF THREE

Oh, how I should love to expand on the implications of His resurrection at this moment; however, we are required to stay with the third law. The Lord Jesus actually and literally fulfilled the

Father's Promise and completed all that was in His heart. The redemptive act happened in eternity and Christ walked it out in time. Now, in time, we are admonished to become intimately involved in the "clean up" of all that happened during this redemptive act.

This Kingdom offer is nothing less than Father's invitation to us to make the "Kingdom happening" to be our priority. Seek this first, says Jesus, and you will see Him add to you all that is needed and necessary (Matthew 6:33). Our job is the declaration and proclamation of the redemptive act itself. We are to mentor the nations in all that He taught us: clean up the confusion; speak to the religious crazies; tell the intended purpose, *boulema*, Father's affectionate purpose and deliberate resolve.

We are, in a true, biblical sense, responsible to proclaim and embrace all three of the laws. Father God certainly did plan carefully. He really did accomplish His intended task. Now, He is making sure the "clean up" goes as it was planned before the foundation of the world. Everything has been carefully planned, successfully executed, and placed in our hands. Sell it all and buy the field in which this treasure can be found (Matthew 13:44). Trade your pearls for the single purpose of not allowing what He has accomplished thus far to capture you in some past happening. The "clean up" is far from over. The issues are increasing complex. The challenges may demand our laying down our physical life. This awakening is urgent. The issues are coming clear. All three of the "laws" have been successfully accomplished and scripturally presented by "the Lamb that was slain before the foundation of the world"(Revelation 13:8).

Welcome to the authentic Kingdom. We are discovering that progressively Father seeks to gain from each of us that which He cannot create: unforced Love that seeks to give Him our heart and our soul with all of its emotions as well as our fallen mind-set. We discover ourselves willing to give Him our strength, willing to walk with Him in weakness. This is one of the themes of Paul's letter to the Philippian believers.

The Mirror bible seeks to incorporate in its translation of the Greek, the full implications of the Law of Three. When Paul writes to the Philippian believers, we will discover ourselves enabled to grasp our actual origin as the act of the Father given in Christ before the world was formed. Paul, in sync with Jesus, writes from this eternal perspective that we seem to be just now discovering and incorporating.

Before you proceed, take the time and effort to examine all 10 of these rather dramatic "preparation" scriptures. All ten are presented in biblical sequence. The purpose is to grasp our birth in Him. Allow them to communicate and impart a fresh eternal perspective. When these have been absorbed and partially digested, read with care the fresh insights into the remarkable epistle to the Philippian believers.

10 BIBLICAL "FOUNDATION OF THE WORLD"

SCRIPTURES (Blue Letter Bible)

"[This was] to fulfill what was spoken through the prophet: 'I will open my mouth in parables; I will utter things hidden since the foundation of the world.'" (Mat 13:35).

"Then the King will say to those on His right, 'Come, you who are blessed of My Father, inherit the kingdom prepared for you from the foundation of the world'" (Mat 25:34).

"So that the blood of all the prophets, shed since the foundation of the world, may be charged against this generation" (Luk 11:50).

"Father, I desire that they also, whom You have given Me, be with Me where I am, so that they may see My glory which You have given Me, for You loved Me before the foundation of the world" (Jhn 17:24).

"Just as He chose us in Him before the foundation of the world, that we would be holy and blameless before Him. In love." (Eph 1:4)

"For we who have believed enter that rest, just as He has said, 'As I swore in my wrath, they shall not enter my rest,' although His works were finished from the foundation of the world" (Heb 4:3).

"Otherwise, He would have needed to suffer often since <u>the foundation of the world</u>; but now once at the consummation of the ages He has been manifested to put away sin by the sacrifice of Himself" (Heb 9:26).

"For He was foreknown before <u>the foundation of the world</u>, but has appeared in these last times for the sake of you" (1Pe 1:20).

"All who dwell on the earth will worship him, [everyone] whose name has not been written from <u>the foundation of the world</u> in the book of life of the Lamb who has been slain" (Rev 13:8).

"The beast that you saw was, and is not, and is about to come up out of the abyss and go to destruction. And those who dwell on the earth, whose name has not been written in the book of life from <u>the foundation of the world</u>, will wonder when they see the beast, that he was and is not and will come" (Rev 17:8).

The Epistle of Philippians, The Mirror Bible

by François du Toit

Introduction to Philippians:

Paul, Silas, Timothy and Luke visited Philippe and founded the first church in Europe on Paul's second missionary journey around A.D. 50 (Acts 16:11-40).

This letter was written in about 61 A.D. from Rome while Paul was under house arrest.

He writes from a place of strength and joy to encourage his dear friends in Philippi, who were also facing many contradictions.

Phil 1:20 My immediate circumstances do not distract from my message! I am convinced that our conversation now and always will continue to give accurate account of the magnificence of Christ. The message is incarnate in me; whether I live or die, it makes no difference.

Phil 1:21 Christ defines my life; death cannot threaten or diminish that.

Phil 2:12 "Not only in my presence but much more in my absence..." Paul knew that he would be more present in his message than in his person! Ministry success is not measured by how many partners you can congregate, but how absent you can preach yourself!

Phil 3:1 The conclusion of your faith is extreme gladness in the Lord. He is your constant reference to bliss! I am not just saying this to be repetitive; joy is your fortress! There is no safer place to be, but to be ecstatically happy!

Paul encourages them not to allow religion to distract from the delight of romance.

Phil 3:7 The sum total of my religious pedigree and sincere devotion amounts to zero! What we have been gifted with in Christ has reduced what once seemed so important, to meaningless information. To esteem the law is to your loss! Faith is your profit.

Phil 3:8 In fact, I have come to the conclusion that every association I have had with that which defined me before as a devout Jew, is by far eclipsed by what I have gained in knowing the Messiah. Jesus Christ and his masterful redemption define me now. Religion is like dog pooh; and it stinks, avoid stepping in it!

Phil 4:4 Joy is not a luxury option; joy is your constant! Your union in the Lord is your permanent source of delight; so I might as well say it again, rejoice in the Lord always!

Phil 4:6 Let no anxiety about anything ¹distract you!

Phil 4:11 I have discovered my "I am-ness" and found that I am fully ¹self sufficient, whatever the circumstance. *(Self sufficient, [1]**autarkes**, self complacent, the feeling you have when you are completely satisfied with yourself.)*

Phil 4:13 In every situation I am strong in the one who empowers me from within to be who I am! *(Paul lived his life in touch with this place within himself. He discovered that the same I am-ness that Jesus walked in, was mirrored in him! I am what I am by the grace of God! 1 Cor 15:10)*

Letter to the Philippians:

1:1 Paul and Timothy address all the Saints in Christ Jesus in Philippi, including your leadership team, both the [1]overseers and the [2]deacons. *(Overseer, [1]**episkopos,** from epi, indicating continues influence upon, and **skopos,** "scope" to see the overall picture, [2]**diakonos,** from **diako**, to run errands, to pursue; see Phil 3:14.)*

1:2 The Father's favor joins our lives inseparably in the Lordship of Jesus Christ.

1:3 The thought of you always inspires me with joy and gratitude to God.

1:4 Praying for you is certainly not a job - it is more like poetry; I joyfully anticipate the outcome of my prayers for you!

1:5 Our blissful participation in everything that the gospel communicates does not age. The fresh-

ness of our first encounter continues to this very day.

1:6 I possess an inward certainty about you, confident that he who is the [1]initiator of the good work within you is also the one who executes its completeness as mirrored in Jesus Christ, who is the light of day. He is the fullness of time. *(Initiator, [1]enarche, to rehearse from the beginning. See Eccl 3:15, "that which has been is now; and that which is to be has already been!")*

1:7 I am not being presumptuous to be this persuaded about you. In the context of our redeemed innocence I cannot think of you any differently; I have you in my heart! Your committed friendship in my imprisonment is of great encouragement to me in our combined defense and confirmation of the gospel. We are in this together! We are joint participants in the same grace. My grace is your grace.

1:8 God knows my intense longing for you! It is with the tender affections of Jesus Christ!

1:9 It is my desire for each one of you, that the realization of [1]love's completeness in you will increasingly burst through all boundaries and that every sphere of your relationship with others will be greatly impacted by your intimate acquaintance with love. *(The word [1]agape is a compound word from ago, which means to lead as a Shepherd leads his sheep,* and **pao**, which means rest! His love leads me into his rest; into the full realization of his finished work! Agape is Psalm 23 in one word. "By the waters of reflection my soul remembers who I am.")

1:10 I urge you to examine this agape-love with the utmost scrutiny, just like when a diamond is viewed in the full sunlight to prove its flawless perfection. I dare you to take love to its ultimate conclusion! There is no offence in love, as evidenced in Jesus Christ who is the light of day. *(If the diamond is flawless to begin with, every possible test will prove its perfection; how someone might respond to love's initiative is not the point. Love's ultimate test was concluded on the cross. Truth does not become true by popular vote; someone's ignorance or indifference cannot change the truth.)*

1:11 You have been fully furnished with the harvest of your redeemed innocence and righteousness for which Jesus Christ labored! This is what the glorious intent of God is all about! Celebrate him!

1:12 I wish to encourage you dear friends that the opposition I face, which was meant to defeat the gospel, has only served to advance it!

1:13 The prison has become my pulpit! All the soldiers in the Governor's guard and everyone involved in the palace have learnt about my message. They know that I am not their prisoner but that I am enclosed in Christ.

1:14 My imprisonment has also persuaded many believers in the Lord to speak the word with fearless courage.

1:15 Some slander the message and others speak with passion and delightful certainty.

1:16 There are those who wish to get mileage out of my predicament for their own agenda.

1:17 Others again are completely love inspired and in full support with me in my defense of the gospel!

1:18 I am thrilled! Christ is the topic of conversation everywhere! Even the negative publicity continues to advertise him!

1:19 I can just see how the Spirit of Jesus Christ, like a [1]conductor of music, takes all of this together with your prayers and turns it into a concert that celebrates salvation! *(The word, [1]epichoregeo, comes from **epi**, a preposition of position, over, in charge, + **chorus**, choir, orchestra, or dance + **ago**, meaning to lead as a Shepherd leads his sheep; thus, the leader of a dance or the conductor of music.)*

1:20 My [1]thoughts are not trapped in my head! They roam free in expectation that I will not be ashamed by any contradiction! My [2]immediate circumstances do not distract from my message! I am convinced that our [2]conversation now and always will continue to give accurate account of the magnificence of Christ. The message is incarnate in me; whether I live or die, it makes no difference. *(The word, [1]apokaradokia is a compound word with 3 parts, apo, away from, kara, head and dokeo, thought. The word [2]parrhesia, from para, a preposition indicating close proximity, a thing proceeding from a sphere of influence, with a suggestion of union of place of residence, to have sprung from its author and giver, originating from, denoting the point from which an action originates, intimate connection; and rhesia, conversation.)*

1:21 Christ defines my life; death cannot threaten or diminish that.

1:22 To be alive now is to feast on the harvest of your faith! I cannot tell when I shall lift up the anchor of the flesh and sail away! It doesn't really matter to me. *(The word, [1]aihreomai, from airo, to lift the anchor and sail away.)*

1:23 I am often torn between these two thoughts. I have this strong yearning to step out of the confines of this body into the immediate embrace of Christ! Can you imagine the awesomeness of that!

1:24 Yet this gospel has my [1]arm twisted and locked behind my back; I am therefore determined to remain in the body for your sakes. *(The word, [1]anagke, suggests to have the arm twisted and locked behind one's back. See 1 Cor 9:16.)*

1:25 I am certain that my time with you will inspire

the happy progress of your pioneering faith!

1:26 The joy of our union in Christ knows no limits! We have so much reason to celebrate! I can just imagine the eruptions of bliss should I be there with you right now in person!

1:27 The [1]one essential thing that would fully engage the focus of your earthly citizenship is the fact that your daily conduct communicates [2]like value and gives context to the gospel of Christ! So whether I am present with you to witness your steadfastness with my own eyes, or absent, our spiritual [3]union and single mindedness will be equally evident. *(The word [1]**monon,** points to that which is singled out as most essential; the word [2]**axios**, means, having the weight of another thing of like value, worth as much. Psyche, Greek, pshuche, suggests consciousness, mental attitude, awareness. Paul desires to express an inseparable togetherness; [3]**sunathleo**, athletic contest. Bicycle racing uses the term peloton; where the riders are strongest and fastest when they ride in the so-called "peloton", which is a densely packed group of riders, sheltering in each others' draft. In a mass-start race, most of the competitors usually end up in one large peloton for most of the race. The word is French, from a term that means rolled up in a ball.)*

1:28 Your brave fearlessness in the face of every kind of obstacle is a sure sign to those who oppose you that their efforts are futile. Your triumphant attitude makes salvation even more apparent. *(There* is no counterfeit; God has no competition! Religion's self-help programs of salvation do not threaten him!)

1:29 Because of the grace that you are gifted with in Christ, whatever you might suffer on behalf of him can never distract from what faith knows to be true about you!

1:30 Our faith is on exhibit in the same public ¹arena; we are not spectators of one another's endurance, but co-witnesses thereof. We mirror one another triumphantly. *(The word, ¹**agon**, refers to the place of contest, the arena or stadium.)*

2:1 In Christ our ¹association is most intimate; we ²articulate his love story; entwined in spirit communion and tender affections. *(The word ¹**parakaleo**, from **para**, a preposition indicating close proximity, a thing proceeding from a sphere of influence, with a suggestion of union of place of residence, to have sprung from its author and giver, originating from, denoting the point from which an action originates, intimate connection, and **kaleo**, to identify by name, to surname. The word ²**paramuthion**, is from **para** + **muthos**, a myth or tale, a story of instruction, told in heart to heart language.)*

2:2 Your Christ mindedness completes my delight! You co-echo the same agape; we are soul mates, resonating the same thoughts.

2:3 No hidden agenda with a compromised mixture of leaven or empty philosophical flattery can

match a mind that genuinely values others above oneself.

2:4 To discover your own completeness in Christ frees you to turn your attention away from yourself to others!

2:5 The way Jesus saw himself is the only valid way to see yourself!

2:6 His being God's equal in form and likeness was official; his Sonship did not steal the limelight from his Father! Neither did his humanity distract from the deity of God!

2:7 His mission however, was not to prove his deity, but to embrace our humanity. Emptied of his reputation as God, he fully embraced our physical human form; born in our resemblance he identified himself as the servant of the human race. His love enslaved him to us!

2:8 And so we have the drama of the cross in context: the man Jesus Christ who is fully God, becomes fully man to the extent of willingly dying humanity's death at the hands of his own creation. He embraced the curse and shame of the lowest kind in dying a criminal's death. *(Thus, through the doorway of humanity's death, he descended into our hellish darkness. See Rev 9:1 and Eph 4:8-10.)*

2:9 From this place of utter humiliation, God

exalted him to the highest rank. God graced Jesus with a Name that is far above every other name. *(Eph 1:20 Do you want to measure the mind and muscle of God? Consider the force which he unleashed in Jesus Christ when he raised him from the dead and forever seated him enthroned as his executive authority in the realm of the heavens. Jesus is God's right hand of power! He was raised up from the deepest dungeons of human despair to the highest region of heavenly bliss! [Also Eph 2:5,6 & 4:8,9] Eph 1:21 Infinitely above all the combined forces of rule, authority, dominion or governments; he is ranked superior to any name that could ever be given to anyone of this age or any age still to come in the eternal future. The name of Jesus endorses his mission as fully accomplished! He is the Savior of the world! Titus 2:11 The grace of God shines as bright as day making the salvation of humanity undeniably visible. See also Eph 3:15, Every family in heaven and on earth originates in him; his is humanity's family name and he remains the authentic identity of every nation.)*

2:10 What his name unveils will persuade every creature of their redemption! Every knee in heaven and upon the earth and under the earth shall bow in spontaneous worship! *(See Isa 45:23 "My own life is the guarantee of my conviction, says the Lord, every knee shall freely bow to me in worship, and every tongue shall spontaneously speak from the same God-inspired source.")*

2:11 Also every tongue will voice and resonate the

same devotion to his unquestionable Lordship as the Redeemer of life! Jesus Christ has glorified God as the Father of creation! This is the ultimate conclusion of the Father's [1]intent! *(The word [1]**doxa,** intent, opinion, often translated, glory. Rev 5:13 And I heard every creature in heaven and on earth and under the earth and in the sea, and all therein, saying, "To him who sits upon the throne and to the Lamb be blessing and honor and glory and might for ever and ever!" See commentary note on Rom 14:11 Paul, here quotes Isaiah 45:23 See verse 20, 22,& 23 "Face me and **be** saved all the ends of the earth! [Note, '**Be saved**!' Not 'become saved!'] I am God your idols are figments of your invention and imagination!" [See 45:20] Isa 45:23 I have sworn by myself; the word of my mouth has begotten righteousness; this cannot be reversed! (See Rom 1:17. The Hebrew word **YATSA** can be translated, begotten like in Judges 8:30] Every knee shall bow to me and every tongue shall echo my oath! [Thus, speak with the same certainty sourced in me!] The Hebrew word, **SHA-BA** means to seven oneself, that is, swear - thus in the Hebrew mind, by repeating a declaration seven times one brings an end to all dispute! See Heb 6:13.16,17.)*

2:12 Considering this amazing outcome of what our faith sees and celebrates, I strongly urge you my darling friends to continue to have your [1]ears tuned to that which inspires your conduct to give full expression to the detail of your own salvation

in a most personal and practical way. See salvation in its earth-shattering awesome and ultimate conclusion. I know that my personal presence encourages you greatly but now I want you to realize an inspiration in my absence that supersedes anything you've known before. This would mean that even if you were never to see my face again or receive another Epistle from me, it will make no difference at all to your faith! *(The success of Paul's ministry was not to enslave people to him but to his gospel! He knew that he would be more present in his message than in his person! Ministry success is not measured by how many partners you can congregate, but by how absent you can preach yourself! The word often translated, obedience, is the word [1]**upoakoo,** to be under the inspired influence of what you hear.)*

2:13 Discover God himself as your inexhaustible inner source; he ignites you with both the desire and energy that matches his own delight!

2:14 Your entire life is a poem; any undercurrent murmuring or argumentative debating would be completely out of place! Do not let such issues disrupt the rhythm of your conversation.

2:15 Your flawless innocence radiates attraction as beacons of light in the midst of a people who have forgotten their true sonship and whose lives have become distorted and perverse. *(In this verse Paul quotes Deut 32:5 from the Greek Septuagint trans-*

lation of the Hebrew text, with reference to Deut 32:4,5 &18. In context God's perfect workmanship as Father of humanity is forgotten; people have become "crooked and perverse" twisted and distorted out of their true pattern of sonship. Deut 32:18 says, "you have forgotten the Rock that begot you and have gotten out of step with the God who [1]*danced with you!" Hebrew,* [1]***khul** *or* **kheel.***)*

2:16 Your lives [1]**echo-exhibit the** [2]**logic of the message of life. You are positioned like the stars in the night sky, superimposed and radiating light, which shining pierces the darkness. Thus you** [3]**confirm the day of the Lord and** [3]**complete my joy! You are my wreath of honor and** [3]**proof that I did not run my race in vain.** *(The word,* [1]***epecho,** *is from* **epi**, *to superimpose, and* **echo**, *to hold, echo resonance. The word of life,* [2]***logos**, *it embodies a conception or idea, thought, logic. The preposition* [3]***eis**, *suggests a point reached in conclusion. See Col 1:29 Your completeness in Christ is not a remote goal, but your immediate reference! My labor now exceeds any zeal that I previously knew under the duty-driven law of willpower. I am laboring beyond the point of exhaustion, striving with intense resolve with all the energy that he mightily inspires within me.)*

2:17 I want you to see my ministry to you as wine poured out upon the altar of your faith. I rejoice in the thought that we drink from the same source and therefore celebrate a mutual joy!

2:18 Whatever you may suffer only concludes in

joy! *(Joy is a bold declaration, in the face of severe danger and suffering, that contradiction does not define us or have the final say in our lives. We know that whether we live or die, our message is unstoppable and that it is conquering the world.)*

2:19 I trust the Lord that I will be able to send Timothy to you soon; this will be to me as if I am there personally with you!

2:20 I have no one here that shares my heart more fully; I know that he will take care of you with utmost concern.

2:21 Sadly there are many in ministry with a selfish agenda

2:22 I do not need to tell you anything about Timothy because you already know his worth! We have labored together in the gospel in the closest possible association; we are like father and son in joint partnership.

2:23 I would like to send him to you immediately, but I am just waiting to see how things here turn out for me.

2:24 I obviously would be very keen to join him shortly! I trust in the Lord for a positive outcome in my trial.

2:25 I feel urgent about sending Epaphrodites to you immediately; he is my brother, fellow-worker and co-campaigner. You initially sent him to help me and now I am returning the favor!

2:26 He longs for you and really misses you. He felt quite distressed when he heard of your concern for him when he was so sick.

2:27 He nearly died but thank God for his mercy, not just for Epaphroditus' sake but for ours also! I cannot imagine the grief we would have suffered had we lost him!

2:28 I am sending him to you without delay; knowing what joy he will be to you is already such a comfort to me!

2:29 The immense value of his life is to be celebrated with a massive bliss-party when he arrives! Oh the joy to love one another in the Lord!

2:30 I so honor his total commitment to the work of Christ; he had no problem to risk his life to serve me on your behalf!

3:1 The conclusion of your faith is extreme gladness in the Lord. He is your constant reference to bliss! I am not just saying this to be repetitive; joy is your fortress! There is no safer place to be, but to be ecstatically happy! *(The joy of Jaweh is your fortress. Nehemiah 8:10.)*

3:2 The circumcision party are the enemies of your faith and freedom! They work with an evil agenda! Be on your guard for them just like you would avoid a vicious hound on the loose! They have their knives in for you!

3:3 We give "circumcision" its true spiritual meaning! Our worship is not defined by anything external that would even remotely resemble the law of works and religious rituals! We worship God in the certainty of our redeemed innocence and rejoice in the finished work of Jesus Christ. Faith-righteousness gives substance to spiritual worship; the flesh occupies the religious mind with its own futile efforts to attain to righteousness. I am convinced that circumcision or any work of the law can add nothing to the righteousness that Jesus secured on our behalf.

3:4 I have more reason than anyone else to rely on my years of diligent and most sincere devotion to Jewish sentiment and rituals. If gaining God's approval had anything to do with striving and personal effort I would beat the best in the business! My pedigree is obvious:

3:5 I received the famous cut when I was 8 days old, exactly as the law prescribed. I am Israeli by birth; the head of my tribe is Benjamin. I am a Hebrew of the Hebrews! In my observance of the law I belonged to the strictest party; I was proud to be a **Pharisee.** *(Rachel was the darling wife of Jacob; she died while giving birth to Benjamin; also the two tribes that* *did not revolt were Benjamin and Judah. By saying that he is a Hebrew of the Hebrews Paul emphasises that his lineage from both parents side was not mixed with any Gentile blood.)*

3:6 The extremities of my fervor were demonstrated in the way I fiercely opposed and persecuted anyone who identified themselves in Christ. *(The so-called Ekklesia.)* **If keeping the law and these credentials could possibly have given me a blameless standing before God, I had it made!**

3:7 The sum total of my religious pedigree and sincere devotion amounts to zero! What we have been gifted with in Christ has reduced what once seemed so important, to meaningless information. To esteem the law is to your loss! Faith is your profit.

3:8 In fact, I have come to the conclusion that every association I have had with that which defined me before as a devout Jew, is by far eclipsed by what I have gained in knowing the Messiah. Jesus Christ and his masterful redemption define me now. Religion is like dog pooh; and it stinks, avoid stepping in it!

3:9 So here I am; found in Christ! I was looking in the wrong place all along! My own duty-and-guilt-driven religious endeavor snared me in the cul-de-sac maze of self-righteousness, sponsored by the law of works! The faith of Christ reveals my iden-

tity; **righteousness defines who God believes that I really am. This righteousness is sourced in God and endorses the authority of faith.** *(Faith is a fairy tale if Jesus is not the substance of it!)*

3:10 Oh to comprehend the dynamic of his resurrection! His resurrection is evidence of our righteousness! In the revelation of God's economy of inclusion, I actually co-suffered with him and co-died together with Christ! *(Because I was already fully represented in his sufferings, his death and resurrection, I am greatly inspired when faced with contradictions now!)*

3:11 When confronted with death, I actually come [1]face to face with my own resurrection! *(The word [1]katantao, from kata + anti, to come to a place over against, opposite another, face to face. 1 Cor 15:18 No resurrection implies no hope for anyone beyond the grave; it makes no difference whether you believed that you were included in Christ's death or not. 1 Cor 15:19 If our hope in Christ was restricted to only benefit us in this life then imagine the severity of our disappointment if it all had to come to an abrupt end when we died. 1 Cor 15:20 However this very moment the risen Christ represents everyone who has ever died; exactly like the first fruit represents the complete harvest. 1 Cor 15:21 The same humanity who died in a man was raised again in a man. 1 Cor 15:22 In Adam all died; in Christ all are made alive.)*

3:12 There may be blurry edges to my [1]compre-

hending the full scope of resurrection life beyond the grave; but I pursue the complete conclusion of co-comprehending and [2]fully grasping exactly that which Jesus Christ knew all along about me when he died my death; and to see me in his faith where I am so perfectly included when he rescued and raised me out of the grasp of death! *(The word, [1]lambano, means to comprehend, to grasp, to identify with. 1 Cor 13:12 To know even as I have always been known! The word [2]katalambano, from kata, which here strengthens the verb lambano, thus to entirely grasp; to come to terms with, to make one's own. The KJV reads, "that I may apprehend that for which also I am apprehended of by Christ Jesus.")*

3:13 I am not boasting about this new-found-righteousness as if I came up with the idea; on the contrary, I have distanced myself from everything the DIY-system of the law of works and willpower previously represented in my reference; now I am fully engaged with that to which the prophetic pointed. Christ is whom we were reaching for all along! Here he is [1]in our face; within our immediate grasp! *(The DIY-system, is the fruit of the 'do it yourself-tree'. The word [1]emprosthen, from en, in, and pros, that which is right in front of me! See Jn 4:26 Mirror "Jesus responded … "I am the One you were longing for.")*

3:14 I have the prize of humanity's redeemed innocence in full view; just like a champion athlete in the public games I refuse to be distracted by anything else. God has ¹invited us in Christ, to lift up our eyes and realize our identity in him. *(The word, ¹**klesis,** invitation, from **kaleo,** to surname, to identify by name. While the law engages one with that which is below, faith captivates our gaze to only see that which is above, where we are co-seated together with Christ in heavenly places! We are identified in him. Col 3:1.)*

3:15 We who have discovered our perfect righteousness have our thoughts anchored in Christ. If you still see yourself as imperfect, God will reveal to you that you are wasting your time to imagine that you can become more accepted and righteous than what you already are!

3:16 So then, let the message of grace set the pace. *(The law is a detour leading nowhere!)*

3:17 You are free to mimic me as we together impact the lives of many others to follow in our footsteps.

3:18 As you know I am often moved to tears talking about these things; I am so passionate about the revelation of humanity's redeemed innocence that it makes no sense to me that there can still be people who oppose this message. Many are openly hostile and indifferent to the cross of Christ.

3:19 Do they not realize that the DIY law-system leads to self-destruction? All their devotion to the god of their religious appetites, endorses their shame; yet they seem to have no problem with it since their minds are seared with [1]sin-consciousness. *("Earthly things" in this case refers to the fallen mindset ruled by a sin-consciousness. See Col 3:1-3, Heb 10:1, 19-22.)*

3:20 Our [1]citizenship is referenced in our joint position with Christ in heavenly places! Heaven is not our goal, it is our [2]starting point! Our understanding is [3]sourced in a Savior; we [4]fully embrace the Lord Jesus Christ! *(The word, [1]**politeuma**, common wealth, our social identity. The word [2]**uparcho**, means to make a beginning, starting point. The word translated source is the word, [3]**ek**. To fully embrace, [4]**apekdechomai**, from **apo**, away from [that which defined me before] and **ek**, out of, source; and **dechomai**, to take into ones hands to accept whole heartedly, to fully embrace)*

3:21 The salvation that Jesus is the author of, re-fashions these bodies of clay and elevates us to fully participate in the same pattern of his heavenly glory! The severe contradiction that we might often face in the frailty of the flesh, is by far surpassed by the glorious splendor displayed in his human body raised from the dead; according to the working of God's dynamic power he imprints the mirror pattern of his likeness in us. Thus he subdues all things to himself. *(Paul's quest to fully comprehend the power of the resurrection (3:10) is consistent with his prayer in Eph 1:19 I pray that you will understand beyond all comparison the magnitude of his mighty power at work*

*¹in us who believe. Faith reveals how enormously advantaged we are in Christ. [The preposition ¹**eis**, speaks of a point reached in conclusion.] Eph 1:20 It is the same dynamic energy which God unleashed in Christ when he raised him from the dead and forever established him in the power of his own right hand in the realm of the heavens. Eph 1:21 Infinitely above all the combined forces of rule, authority, dominion, or governments; he is ranked superior to any name that could ever be given to anyone of this age or any age still to come in the eternal future. Eph 1:22 I want you to see this: he subjected all these powers under his feet. He towers head and shoulders above everything. He is the head; Eph 1:23 the ¹church is his body. The completeness of his being that fills all in all resides in us! God cannot make himself more visible or exhibit himself more accurately. [The word, ¹Ekklesia, comes from ek, a preposition always denoting origin, and klesia from kaleo, to identify by name, to surname; thus the "church" is his redeemed image and likeness in humanity.]*

See again Phil 2:6 His being God's equal in form and likeness was official; his sonship did not steal the limelight from his Father! Neither did his humanity distract from the deity of God! Phil 2:7 His mission however, was not to prove his deity but to embrace our humanity. He emptied himself into a physical human form; born in our resemblance he identified himself as the servant of the human race. His love enslaved him to us! Phil 2:8 And so we have the drama of the cross in context: the man

Jesus Christ who is fully God, becomes fully man to the extent of willingly dying humanity's death at the hands of his own creation. He embraced the curse and shame of the lowest kind in dying a criminal's death. Phil 2:9 From this place of utter humiliation, God exalted him to the highest rank. God graced Jesus with a Name that is far [1]above as well as equally representative of every other name; [The word, super, means above, also instead, or for the sake of. The name of Jesus endorses his mission as fully accomplished! He is the Savior of the world! See also Eph 3:15, Every family in heaven and on earth originates in him; his is humanity's family name and he remains the authentic identity of every nation.] Phil 2:10 What his name unveils will persuade every creature of their redemption! Every knee in heaven and upon the earth and under the earth shall bow in spontaneous worship! Eph 4:8 Scripture confirms that he led us as trophies in his triumphant procession on high; he [1]repossessed his gift (likeness) in humanity. (See Ephesians 2:6, We are also elevated in his ascension to be equally welcome in the throne room of the heavenly realm where we are now seated together with him in his authority. Quote from the Hebrew text, Ps 68:18, [1]lakachta mattanoth baadam, thou hast taken gifts in human form, in Adam. [The gifts which Jesus Christ distributes to us he has received in us, in and by virtue of his incarnation. Commentary by Adam Clarke.] We were born anew in his resurrection. 1 Pet 1:3, Hos 6:2.)

4:1 Now in the light of all this, I am sure that you can appreciate what enormous delight you are to me! My precious friends, you are my trophy and my joy! Just as you have been doing, continue to stand immovably strong in the Lord!

4:2 Your [1]source defines you by name! Dear [2]Eodias and [3]Syntyche, let me remind you of the meanings of your names! Engage your thoughts to follow the direct and easy way of grace; then you will together fulfill your mission in the Lord without distraction. *(The word, [1]parakaleo, comes from para, a preposition indicating close proximity, a thing proceeding from a sphere of influence, with a suggestion of union of place of residence, to have sprung from its author and giver, originating from, denoting the point from which an action originates, intimate connection; and kaleo, meaning to identify by name, to surname. The word [2]eudias, from eu, good, and odos, a road, thus a prosperous and expeditious journey, to lead by a direct and easy way; [3]suntuche, from sun, together with, and tugchanō, to hit the mark; of one discharging a javelin or arrow)*

4:3 Suzegos, you are the meaning of your name to me; my trustworthy yoke fellow! Associate yourself closely with these ladies who have been my fellow athletes in the gospel! Also Clement as well as all my other colleagues - I have their names on record in the book of life! *(Paul has all his friends names on record! [See Romans 16:1-23] Zoe life as defined in Christ has given such rich meaning to proper names. Su-*

zugos, meaning yoke-fellow. At Philippi, women were the first hearers of the Gospel, and Lydia the first convert. Acts 16:13-15. **Clement**, clear skies, bright and sunny weather. Paul whose own name was changed from, **Sheol**, meaning dark underworld, to **Pao**, rest, appreciates the meaning of proper names. He calls Peter, Kefas which is the Aramaic for Petros, to deliberately steer away from the more familiar sound of Petros, thus he specifically emphasizes the meaning of his name. The rock foundation of God's Ekklesia. In Mat 16 Jesus identifies Simon, the son of Jonah by a new name, Petros; and upon this revelation, that the son of man is the son of God the Ekklesia is built!)

4:4 Joy is not a luxury option; joy is your constant! Your union in the Lord is your permanent source of delight; so I might as well say it again, rejoice in the Lord always!

4:5 Show perfect [1]courtesy towards all people! The Lord is not nearer to some than what he is to others! *(Courtesy, [1]epieikes, from epi, indicating continues influence upon, and eikos, reasonable, courteous. This is exactly Paul's attitude towards the idol worshipping Greek philosophers in Acts 17:27,28. See also Titus 3:3. Your joy makes the gospel visible! Every definition of distance is cancelled!)*

4:6 Let no anxiety about anything [1]distract you! Rather translate moments into prayerful worship, and soak your requests in gratitude before God!

*(The word [1]**merimnao**, anxiety, through the idea of distraction, from **meritzo**, to divide. Your requests do not surprise God; he knows your thoughts from afar and is acquainted with all your ways; yet he delights in your conversation and childlike trust! Song of Songs 2:14; Mat 6:8.)*

4:7 And in this place of worship and gratitude you will witness how the peace of God within you echoes the awareness of your oneness in Christ Jesus beyond the reach of any thought that could possibly unsettle you. *(uperecho)* **Just like the [1]sentry guard secures a city, watching out in advance for the first signs of any possible threat, your hearts' deepest feelings and the tranquility of your thoughts are fully guarded there.** *(This peace is not measured by external circumstances, it is residing deeply in the innermost parts of your being. We are not talking about a fragile sense of peace that can easily be disturbed; one that we have to fabricate ourselves; this is God's peace; the peace that God himself enjoys!)*

4:8 Now let this be your conclusive [1]reasoning: consider that which is [2]true about everyone as evidenced in Christ. Live [3]overwhelmed by God's opinion of you! Acquaint yourselves with the revelation of [4]righteousness; realize God's likeness in you. Make it your business to declare humanity's redeemed [5]innocence. Think [6]friendship. Discover how [7]famous everyone is in the light of the gospel; humanity is in God's limelight! Ponder how [8]elevated you

are in Christ. Study [9]**stories that celebrate life.** *(See Col 3:3, "Engage your thoughts with throne room realities where we are co-seated together with Christ!" The word* [1]***logitsomai*** *suggests a logical reasoning by taking everything into account;* [2]***alethes****, means that which was hidden, but is now uncovered; In Eph 3:21 Paul speaks about the truth as it is embodied in Jesus. The word overwhelmed is,* [3]***semnos****, from **sebomai***, to revere, to adore. The word for righteousness is* [4]***dikaios****, from **dikay***, two parties finding likeness in each other, where there is no sense of inferiority, suspicion, blame, regret or pressure to perform. The gospel is the revelation of the righteousness of God; it declares how God succeeded to put humanity right with him. It is about what God did right, not what Adam did wrong. See Rom 1:17. The word* [5]***hagnos*** *speaks of blameless innocence. The word* [6]***prophileo****, is exactly what it says, pro-friendship. The English word for famous is derived from the Greek word* [7]***euphemos****, from **eu***, well done, good and **phemos***; it means to be in the lime light, from **phao***, to shine; Jesus said, "you are the light of the world." Just like a city set on a hill, your light cannot be hid. The word* [8]***arete****, is often translated, virtue, from **airo***, to raise up, to elevate;* [9]***epainos****, commendable, praise worthy, from **epi***, indicating continual influence upon, and **ainos***, story.)*

4:9 These things are consistent with all that I teach and live; you can confidently practice what you hear and see in me. The peace that inevitably follows this lifestyle is more than a fuzzy feeling; this

is God himself endorsing our oneness.

4:10 I am so happy in the Lord that after all this time you have shown such revived concern in my well-being. It is refreshing to know your support, even though you did not recently have the opportunity to express it.

4:11 Hey, don't get me wrong, I am not hinting for funding! I have discovered my "I am-ness" and found that I am fully ¹self sufficient, whatever the circumstance. *(Self sufficient, ¹**autarkes**, self complacent, the feeling you have when you are completely satisfied with yourself.)*

4:12 I am not defined by abuse or abundance! It might be a different day and a different place, but the secret remains the same; whether I am facing a feast or a fast, a fountain or famine. *(Abundance is not a sign of God's goodness; neither is lack a sign of his absence! "Righteousness by his (God's) faith defines life." The good news is the fact that the Cross of Christ was a success. God rescued the life of our design; he redeemed our innocence. Humanity would never again be judged righteous or unrighteous by their own ability to obey moral laws! It is not about what someone must or must not do but about what Jesus has done! It is from faith to faith, and not a person's good or bad behavior or circumstances interpreted as a blessing or a curse [Hab 2:4]. Instead of reading the curse when disaster strikes, Habakkuk realizes that the Promise out-dates performance as the basis to* humanity's acquittal. Deuteronomy 28 would no longer be the motivation or the measure of right or wrong behavior! "Though the fig trees do not blossom, nor fruit be on the vines, the produce of the olive fail and the fields yield no food, the flock be cut off from the fold and there be no herd in the stalls, yet I will rejoice in the Lord, I will joy in the God of my salvation. God, the Lord, is my strength; he makes my feet like hinds' feet, he makes me tread upon my high places [Hab 3:17-19 RSV]. "Look away [from the law of works] to Jesus; he is the Author and finisher of faith." [Heb 12:1]. See Rom 1:17.)*

4:13 In every situation I am strong in the one who empowers me from within to be who I am! *(Paul lived his life in touch with this place within himself. He discovered that the same I am-ness that Jesus walked in, was mirrored in him! I am what I am by the grace of God! Christ in me, mirrors Christ in you! Phil 2:12, "Not only in my presence but much more in my absence! Col 1:27 In us God desires to exhibit the priceless treasure of Christ's indwelling; every nation will recognize him as in a mirror! The unveiling of Christ in human life completes humanity's every expectation. He is not hiding in history, or in outer space nor in the future, neither in the pages of scripture, he is merely mirrored there to be unveiled within you. [Mt 13:44, Gal 1:15, 16.])*

4:14 Now I am not saying that I did not need or appreciate your help! Your joint participation in my difficult times was like beautiful poetry to me!

4:15 You and I know very well that your initial encounter with the gospel inspired you to partner with me in the wonderful rhythm of giving and receiving. Your generosity then financed my trip in and out of Macedonia! No other church did what you did. *(Paul visited Thessalonica and Berea, about 12 years before this epistle was written. Acts 17: 1-14.)*

4:16 You also helped me several times in Thessalonica.

4:17 I am not reminding you of your gifts for any other reason but to encourage you to realize the abundant harvest in the word that you are a living epistle of. *(Greek, the fruit of "your word.")*

4:18 This letter is my official [1]receipt to you, proving that my capacity is filled to the brim! I am bursting at the seams indulging in your gifts that Epaphrodites brought! Your generosity celebrates God's pleasure like a sweet perfume poured out on the altar of your love for me. *(The word [1]apecho here is used as a commercial term meaning to receive a sum in full and give a receipt for it. From apo and echo, to hold; in this context the preposition apo with the accusative denotes correspondence of the contents to the capacity; of the possession to the desire. J.B. Lightfoot)*

4:19 My God shall also abundantly fill every nook and cranny to overflowing in all areas of your lives. The wealth of his dream come true in Christ Jesus measures his generosity towards you!

4:20 For countless ages upon ages God will be celebrated as our Father. We are his glory! Most certainly!

4:21 Embrace every saint in Christ Jesus on our behalf; the friends with me embrace you!

4:22 All the Saints, especially those within the household of Caesar greet you dearly!

4:23 The grace that Jesus Christ embodies embraces you in your spirit.

LIFECHANGERS ®

P.O. Box 3709 ❖ Cookeville, TN 38502
931.520.3730 ❖ lc@lifechangers.org

LIFECHANGERS®

P.O. Box 3709 ❖ Cookeville, TN 38502
931.520.3730 ❖ lc@lifechangers.org

www.ingramcontent.com/pod-product-compliance
Lightning Source LLC
Chambersburg PA
CBHW071748020426
42331CB00008B/2231